How to Write a Research Dissertation

Essential Guidance in Getting Started for Undergraduates and Postgraduates

Frank Rennie & Keith Smyth

CREDITS

Published as an e-textbook by eTIPS (a partnership between The Educational Development Unit of The University of the Highlands and Islands, Lews Castle College UHI and Edinburgh Napier University) as part of the Jisc 'Institution as e-textbook publisher' project.

FRANK RENNIE & KEITH SMYTH

CONTENTS

COMPANION WEBSITE

For free learning resources linked to this e-textbook
go to **www.etextbooks.ac.uk/dissertation**

1 WHAT IS RESEARCH AND WHY DO IT?

Objectives

The objective of this chapter is to obtain an appreciation of the nature of systematic academic research, and the comparisons with casual investigation. Also, to begin to relate research issues to the practical application of problem-solving (and a general contribution to society).

Key Points

Due to the fact that research is conducted in the search for answers and solutions as yet unknown, (in fact sometimes the research questions themselves may be quite indistinct) there are many different views of what constitutes research, and some of these view may appear contradictory.

Research can be considered as "systematic investigation towards increasing the sum of human knowledge" (Chambers Dictionary).

or

"Careful search or inquiry... to discover new or collate old facts etc. by scientific study of a subject, course of critical investigation." (Oxford English Dictionary).

In short, research can be considered as a structured investigation into a subject, the aim of which is to add knowledge to that subject and/or to illuminate the subject from a different perspective.

There are several different types of research, and these may be conducted for different reasons, for example:

- 'pure' or exploratory research (basic investigation of an issue for its own sake)

- descriptive, explanatory, and evaluation research

- applied research (investigation directed towards solving a particular problem)

- consultancies (the application of existing knowledge and skills to solve problems presented by a client.)

- strategic research (aimed at providing reasoned options for future policy and planning)

- market research (investigation of consumer choices and purchasing decisions).

- covert and adversarial research

- participatory and collaborative research (in which the subjects share in the investigative process)

- action research (which revolves in a cycle of investigation-action-reflection)

- problem-based research (which, by definition, starts with a specific problem).

An important consideration, both of the type and the quality of research, stems from an understanding of the nature of the motivations of the researcher. This may derive from the role of the researcher as a detached observer, or as an active participant seeking change, or more commonly as a mixture of these types.

The success and quality of a research project frequently depends upon the level of originality which is embodied in the work - this may be original ideas, methods, approaches, and/or means of interpreting the data - but this can also be very difficult to define precisely.

Your research project(s) will also be affected by the clients/subjects/objects which are the focus of your research. An obvious example is that support for your research may be withdrawn if you deliberately set out to humiliate, debunk, or otherwise dismiss or discredit the beliefs and values of your client group. Care is therefore required in the design of research projects.

Optional Activity

You should now consider opening a 'research journal' to record your thoughts for your own dissertation topic. At some stage soon you will want to share these with your research supervisor, and taking regular, structured notes can help to keep track of your ideas and to formulate them more exactly.

Background Reading

Blaxter, L., Hughes, C., and Tight, M. (2010) How to research (4th Edition). The Open University Press - Chapter 1

Bryman, A. (2012) Social Research Methods (4th Edition) Oxford University Press.

[The introductory guide to this book is a good place to start for this topic.]

Murray, R. (2002) How to write a thesis. Open University Press.

2 PLANNING RESEARCH

Objectives

The key point is to consider the stages and general planning of research projects, and to relate these to the programme of study of individual students.

Key Points

A fundamental progression in the development of a research programme is the move from a general statement of research interest covering a wide subject area, to a more specific research question or a hypothesis. This is followed by a dissection of the research question into separate queries, and matching these with a coherent methodology which might help to provide some answers. You need to carefully plan this process, it does not just happen.

This process is not linear - there is not necessarily any end position, as you might simply be led to a more specific and/or different list of research questions.

There are some common aspects which link all good research projects:

- The identification of the problem or research need must be clear and concise.

- Clear identification of the problem or research area provokes specific questions to answer.

- The problem or area for research can be identified within the existing literature.

- The research project should contribute something original or a new perspective on knowledge.

- 'Solving' the research problem or need should have potential significance or importance.

- The research project is achievable within time and budget constraints.

- There is sufficient information (data) to allow meaningful study & comparisons.

The investigation of the problem or the issue to be researched can be tested against a repeatable methodology. Failure of any one of these conditions might cause the research project to flounder, but even if they all go well there is no guarantee of your research project producing a monumental international breakthrough. The nature of research is that we are starting off from a position of relative ignorance, and by eliminating false trails we can proceed to provide answers to increasingly more specific and complex questions. By taking these incremental successes together, we can provide better answers for the large, complicated, and multi-dimensional problems in the future.

A key element of success in the planning of a research project is the adoption of an appropriate methodology for solving each part of the puzzle. The choice of the general research topic, and even the specific areas of investigation can be considered as working titles which can be refined with time and increasing knowledge, but the adoption of an inappropriate methodological approach will usually lead to the collection of data which will not contribute significantly to solving the problem which you have set.

Perhaps the most common complaint that students voice is that they "haven't got enough time" to complete their research dissertation. While they may feel this to be the case, they are almost always wrong. Student research projects are normally clearly defined by the institution to fit with standard formats; for instance, 6-9 months for an Honours undergraduate study; 3-9 months for a taught Masters;1-2 years for a Masters by research; and 3-4 years for a doctorate by research (these time-frames may be extended for part-time study). This means that, from the outset, the student is made aware of the time limitations and must prepare to deliver the dissertation within that time frame. This will need careful planning, and monitoring to ensure that the plan works as it is intended (or that ongoing adjustments can be made to react to changing circumstances). When a plan is faulty, or where poor monitoring and re-adjustment fails to compensate for problems or delays, this is when students complain that they are "running out of time".

The moral is clear. From the early days of your research dissertation activities, you need to develop a clear time-table to guide your work. Perhaps you can identify the key dates – project start, data collection, submission date – and build your other activities around these deadlines. As with most other aspects of a dissertation, there is no fixed blueprint for how you allocate your workload, and this will vary between subject areas, academic level, prior knowledge of the topic, and other aspects such as seasonal factors or the availability of key informants. As a very rough guide, you might think about three roughly equal phases, corresponding to 1) background, introduction and literature review; 2) data collection and analysis; 3) writing, conclusions and 'finishing off' your dissertation. Of course, most research projects will require you to engage in multiple tasks at any one time, so you will need to overlap these phases – read, write, read some more, gather some data, write some more, and so on, until the patchwork mosaic of your work is completed and it reads like a smoothly-flowing piece of literature.

In planning your research you will need to decide exactly how you will gather your data, and this in itself can have important implications in identifying the ethical considerations that are relevant to your project. See Chapter 5 Methods of Research for further guidance.

Optional Activity

Read again the 'plan this process' link above. Construct you own research plan on this model. You will want to use this as the basis for the information you will include in your research project dissertation. You should share your plan with your research supervisor, and with your fellow students if appropriate, to raise questions, clarify your ideas, and generally inform others of your progress in thinking about your project.

Developing a Research Plan

Write out a general statement on your topic or question of interest.

- Start to read the literature surrounding this topic.

- Consult with friends and/or colleagues to clarify the key concepts.

- Try to formulate some specific research questions.

What do you want to know?

- Try to identify the target area and/or population which is to be the subject of your study.

- Try to identify a general strategy for the collection of your data, what data do you need?

- Compare your investigation strategy with other possible methods of research.

- Select the technique(s) which you will use to collect the data.

- Pilot your research methods on a small sample population.

- Evaluate the success of your pilot.

- Modify your techniques (if necessary) and plan a time frame for completion.

- Collect and begin to analyse your data.

- Report your results.

- Analyse and interpret your results.

- Present project conclusions and options for further research.

Statement of Research Interest

First, decide upon a general statement of your research interest. This statement should be sufficiently broad to enable you to explore a number of related areas of interest, and at the same time it has to be focused enough not spread your energy too thinly. Start with a broad topic, such as one of the following statements, then make a list of questions which will help you to define, describe, and subdivide this topic into specific areas for further investigation. Write lots of questions in your research notebook. Some of these will be relatively easy and quick to answer (perhaps a specific definition) and others will remain unanswered even when you are completely finished your project. When you have a lot of questions you can begin to organise them into related clusters and sort them into a level of priority to help inform your research.

- I am interested in the growth of tourism in the X area.

- I am interested in the links between farm diversification and nature conservation.

- I am interested in the role of women in supporting voluntary organisations.

- I am interested in the economics of horticulture products for local consumption.

- I am interested in the attitudes of local business managers towards teleworking.

- I am interested in the comparisons of local health provision between area X and area Y.

- I am interested in discovering exactly how government policy affects SME development.

- I am interested in effect of Objective 1 funding on the fishing industry.

- I am interested in the impact of the LEADER programme in European community development.

- I am interested in why doctors want to work in rural areas.

- I am interested in the importance of fish farming in the rural economy.

- I am interested in opportunities for distance education in remote areas.

- I am interested in the potential use of the internet in rural marketing.

Following these main questions, there will be an almost infinite number of sub-questions to consider. By linking these questions together logically and systematically you can begin to develop an idea on how to plan your research and where to start.

Some Examples of possible Dissertation Titles

- Kershader: A project report on a crofting township with reference to the District of Pairc, Isle of Lewis

- What is the potential for a marine-based eco-tourism facility in the Shetland Islands?

- The benefits and uses of renewable energy in rural areas

- Implementation of Agenda 21 in the Orkney

- What has been the impact of European financial assistance to the voluntary sector in the Western Isles?

- The future of rural tourism: Scotland and Ireland

- PESCA in Western Scotland and Ireland

- Local Exchange Trading Mechanisms: Examples from the Highland Region

- Community Development: Education and empowerment

- Towards a Local Biodiversity Action plan for Easter Ross

- How Objective 1 funding influences sustainable development

- The development of interpretive visitor centres in the Western Isles 1995 to 1999

- Alternative agriculture in Caithness

- Traditional music as a tool for rural development

- A comparative study of small business development in Ireland and Scotland

- The history and importance of land use changes in the Zzzz Region, Scotland

- The influence of local animators in stimulating community development

- Economic and social strategies for agricultural diversification in small islands

- The impact of agricultural support for environmental management in Norway

- A history of the X development organisation and its significance for regional development

- The influence of indigenous culture in the promotion of local tourism attractions.

- A study of the roles of voluntary organisations in the development of rural areas.

- Eco-tourism as a strategy for the development of the XYZ area, Scotland

- The management of environmentally protected areas for social and economic development

Optional Activity

Visit the companion website
www.etextbooks.ac.uk/dissertation
to view more resources.

You might also want to take a look at the additional documentation on the website which may also be of use to you.

Background Reading

Blaxter, L., Hughes, C., and Tight, M. (2010) How to research (4th Edition). The Open University Press - Chapter 2

Bryman, A. (2012) Social Research Methods (4th Edition) Oxford University Press. - Chapters 1 to 3

FRANK RENNIE & KEITH SMYTH

3 ETHICS IN RESEARCH

Objectives

This session outlines some of the main issues and concerns relating to the moral and ethical aspects of undertaking research projects and to consider the evaluation of quality.

Key Points

Up until the previous generation to our own, the collection of scientific data (science or social science) was largely considered to be value-neutral. More recently, however, concerns have been raised as to whether this is always the case, especially with reference to the subsequent use of research results. The use (or misuse) or these results may make the process of undertaking the research process 'unethical' if for example:

- the data is released into the public sphere without the knowledge and/or consent of the participants;

- if this knowledge is used inappropriately, such as to injure people.

Issues relating to ethical activities include:

- **Confidentiality** – generally important, even in non-sensitive cases. Many people may be reluctant to give any information at all in the fear that there may be some repercussions.

- **Consent** – this involves openness when dealing with informants and interviewees, for example there should normally be no attempt to tape or video record evidence without the permission of the participants.

- **Privacy** – sometimes this is an issue when investigating opinions and/or attitudes and personal behaviour. Care is needed to restrict investigation to areas which are relevant and necessary to the study.

- **Integrity** – some informants may agree to comment "off the record", and in doing so could provide extremely useful background information for your study. Due to the fact that it is informal, however, this source should not be utilised, and the information treated sceptically until independent confirmation can be substantiated.

- **Reporting constraints** – this might become an issue of censorship, or even self-censorship, particularly where for example publication may cause offence and/or alienate participants or colleagues. There may also be a dilemma when faced with apparently unpalatable results which do not "fit in" with anticipated (preferred?) results.

At the final audit, ethical issues cannot be legislated for, and are usually as much of a moral concern as a technical problem for diligent researchers. Short-cuts and duplicity will inevitably lead to an unsuccessful project with insufficient and/or inappropriate results for interpretation.

On the whole, it is much better to complete a smaller, less ambitious study which has a solid integrity, than to attempt a big study superficially – or to compromise honesty in order to make the results "look better".

Whether you include a special section in your final report or not, you should always conduct your own evaluation of your research projects. A number of simple evaluation techniques could be included in your working methodology, thereby ensuring a built-in quality control for your data gathering. A self-critical examination will help you to improve aspects of good practice, and will hopefully prevent you from making too many repeated errors.

4 EVALUATION OF RESEARCH

Objectives

To understand the importance of being able to accurately evaluate the importance of a research project and to identify some of the key indicators used to recognise the strengths and limitations on quality.

Key Points

Evaluation is a natural and integral process of human existence. It is a seamless extension of the process of information collection and interpretation - not an additional operation designed to "pick holes" in the research project. Evaluation is only worthwhile if it is thorough and honest (and if we can learn from it to avoid repeating previous errors and false assumptions).

Evaluation has a developmental function, whether it is a formal or non-formal exercise, and whether the evaluation is internal or external to the group (or individuals) conducting the research. A proper evaluation can be a formidable extension of the data collection and interpretation phases, which can give added credibility to the conclusions and/or methods of the project.

Evaluation is a process which aims to determine the value of an object or a piece of work, and as such it requires targets, goals, and standards against which the values can be measured. Self-evaluation is both more difficult and more rewarding than external (independent) evaluation, but it lays a greater stress upon the identification of legitimate indicators, values, and outcomes (which may of course differ for individual evaluators). It is also more open to criticisms of self-interest, a lack of rigour, and a bias towards vested interests (your own!) though in practice self-criticism can often be more scathing than that of colleagues. For these reasons it is important that self-evaluation is not only scrupulously objective (impartial) but also that it is seen to be so.

Sometimes an evaluation may be a self-regulatory exercise, by which researchers aim to compare their work with similar initiatives (perhaps against recognised standards) in an attempt to learn from their own experience (i.e. "how could I do it better next time?") Other types of evaluation will be seen as a necessary prerequisite to ensure the continued support of the funders and/or for the researcher(s) to achieve or maintain a high level of credibility among colleagues. Either way, the agreement on what aspects are to be evaluated, and what standards and conclusions are considered to be acceptable, will be critical to the credibility and value of the evaluation process itself.

An ideal research project would set out in advance the parameters which it is trying to investigate, clearly identifying the criteria for the success of every stage of the investigation. The evaluation process then becomes a straightforward comparison of "before-and-after", with a commentary on the perceived reasons for the level(s) of success. In practice, this very rarely happens, as the research process, by definition, is an exploration of the unknown - which produces the frustrations, excitement, and fascination which makes research so addictive.

Optional Activity

Visit the companion website
www.etextbooks.ac.uk/dissertation
to view more resources.

Background Reading

Blaxter, L., Hughes, C., and Tight, M. (2010) How to research (4th Edition). The Open University Press - Chapter 6

Bryman, A. (2012) Social Research Methods (4th Edition) Oxford University Press.

– Chapter 5 gives useful details of ethics in social science research

Clarke, A. (1999) Evaluation Research: An introduction to principles, methods and practice. Sage Publications

5 INFORMATION IN RESEARCH

Objectives

A fundamental need is to consider ways in which information may be used in the research process in order to draw conclusions from complex data.

Key Points

The main information issues in research resolve around the collection, processing, and the interpretation of data. Each of these aspects may have several, widely different, variations. In addition, the collection of information may be strongly influenced by access issues in which some information, or some types of information may be difficult, sensitive, (or impossible) to obtain. This may influence both the type (extent) of the research project and also the methodology which is used to gather the raw information. (It may also, have a strong influence on the results and the interpretation(s)

There is a big difference between the styles of collection, display, and interpretation of data which is textual, as opposed to data which is numerical in its format. Numerical information may imply a greater degree of measurability of the basic information, but this may be compensated for by a relative lack of richness in the detail, whereas textual material may supply a rich variety of qualitative information which is difficult to precisely measure or quantify. (These are generalisations of course.)

Thirdly, there is a substantial difference in the nature of research which utilises primary information (i.e. data gathered from questionnaires, interviews, and/or experiments conducted by the researcher) and secondary information, which is gathered by someone else but brought together (synthesised) and perhaps re-interpreted by another researcher. A good example of the use of secondary research is the preparation of an annotated bibliography which you can build up as notes in your research journal. Eventually, you can combine the information in these annotations to create a literature review on your main subject area and use this to introduce the context of your studies through a review of the most important academic writing on the subject. The literature review is used to provide an overview of the published materials on a particular topic or theme, and thereby gain a good impression of the current state of knowledge in this subject area. We will deal with the literature review later

Apart from simply being tidy, there are other good reasons for having efficient means of storage for the data which is collected. First and foremost, it is because you must be able to ensure the retrieval of any part of the data which has been collected at any time - loss of data means at best a loss of clarity of the solution to the research problem - at worst it means drawing the wrong conclusions from very partial evidence. Secondly, good storage systems will allow the researcher to sort and to display the information (which might be a considerable amount) in ways which make it easier to understand and interpret. This might be a key element in the success of a research project which produces controversial conclusions resulting in the necessity of isolating complex data to ensure the repeatability of a line of study or experiment.

In large studies, or in research project which combine different methodologies, there may be a large amount of complex data sets, and it may be necessary to summarise and/or isolate some of the information which is most useful from the general 'background' information. This selection of the primary data (usually when there is too much) may also prove problematic (it may be tempting - but wrong - to ignore results which do not fit neatly with the explanation of your pet theory). This may also lead to problems in the interpretation of results and/or the ability to contrast and compare with other (previous) studies.

A good technique to identify your potential sources of information is to jot down a long list of all the questions that you have – from the simplest to the most difficult – these can then be collected into thematic groups to provide a number of focused areas for deeper investigation.

Another useful idea is to make a list of the sorts of places and/or specific people that might be able to provide you with relevant data to assist your investigations.

Reference management

When you start to conduct a piece of research, and you begin to read relevant academic articles on your subject area, it can seem quite a simple activity to organise them, but as the references mount up, it rapidly becomes quite complex. There are a number of techniques and tools that can be used to ease the management of a large amount of references so that you can always identify and recover any important piece of information.

At the simplest level, some researchers prefer to use old-fashioned index cards – one card per reference, containing the full citation, and perhaps a two-sentence summary of the article that can be useful in the compilation of the literature review. At the next level, a word document can be opened on a computer and each citation added in alphabetic order as the articles have been read. At the end of the project it is a simple matter to print-out a complete reference list (but make sure that you maintain up-to-date back-up copies!). Lastly, there are various software packages (such as RefWorks) some of which are free to download or use (such as Mendeley) which allow you to list, store and/or share your references, and to store notes that you have made in relation to your readings.

There are several websites that compare reference management software (such as on Wikipedia) and list their pros and cons. As with any software package, there needs to be a balance between the set-up time and skills required to get started, versus the overall benefits to your work. On the whole, these are probably more useful for larger projects that run over a number of years where different combinations of citations are re-used and re-configured for different purposes.

Regardless of which system you choose, make sure that it is effective and appropriate for your needs (no need for a sledgehammer to crack a nut!) and start using it to record your references as soon as you start your project. Leaving the organisation of your references to a later date only encourages confusion and extra work.

Optional Activity

In your personal research journal, prepare a short note on:

a) What sort of data do you want and/or need to gather in order to complete your dissertation?

b) Precisely how do you intend to manage your references?

How to Prepare an Annotated Bibliography

What does this mean? An annotated bibliography is ordered list of citations to books, journal articles, and other documents (including, increasingly, World Wide Web locations). Each citation is followed by a brief paragraph (usually around 150 words) which describes and attempts to evaluate the citation.

These annotations are descriptive, but also take a critical view. The purpose of the annotation is to inform the reader of the views of the author(s), their relevance to the topic of research, as well as the clarity of expression and the accuracy of their text. The annotation may also comment upon the quality of the sources cited and the level of authority of the citation.

The preparation of an annotated bibliography requires a range of professional attributes including library retrieval, critical reading, analytical evaluation, concise writing skills, and perhaps information technology competence.

A good annotation to a bibliographic reference should:

- summarise the central theme of the book or article;

- evaluate the conclusions of the reference;

- explain how this work contributes to the topic of your thesis;

- perhaps compare this work with other relevant

works cited.

A sample of an entry in an annotated bibliography (though a little on the short side for a word count) would be as follows:

[extract from Mather and Arden, 1981]

Hunter, J., 1976, The making of the crofting community. John Donald: Edinburgh. This major work traces the evolution of crofting from the early nineteenth century to the land raids and land settlement schemes in parts of the Highlands and Islands in the early twentieth century. The major land-use trends and changes in the Highlands and islands are discussed, and the events leading to the Crofters Act of 1886 are considered in detail.

The aim of the annotated bibliography is to guide your reader through the background literature to your chosen subject in a knowledgeable and balanced manner. At the end of the day it is up to you to select the references which you consider to be most appropriate, and to justify your choice in each annotation.

Some important access issues

There are some general points regarding the access to and the use of information which you must consider when embarking upon any research project. The following points are not prioritised and are not exhaustive - they may vary in their relative importance between different projects and even at different times within the same project.

- A simple, concise statement giving written details of your research ideas, aims, and methods may help as a useful introduction when seeking access or help (e.g. to a library).

- Seek permission to interview / question the staff of an organisation before you approach them. Some organisations have an official channel for dealing with external enquiries, and you are required to use this.

- Before you commence your study, speak to the participants who will be asked to co-operate. If you telephone participants, always establish that it is a convenient time to speak to them.

- Be honest with participants about your research methods. If you are granted a half-hour interview, don't let it drag on for an hour - try to make another appointment when it is more suitable.

- All participants should be offered the chance to remain anonymous. (You must, however, be able to refer to them by a code or number - 'participant 1' - and keep a separate list of identities.)

- Treat all information in the strictest confidence. In some sectors, for example medicine and public finance, you may be required to sign a confidence agreement (such as the Official Secrets Declaration).

- Never use unsubstantiated information until / unless it can be independently proven.

- Offer each interviewee the opportunity to verify their statements when the research is in draft form.

- Be honest with the participants about what will be done with the information which they provide for your research (e.g. is it for your degree project, or a specific client, or for an academic publication).

- Acknowledge all sources of information and support (unless they wish to remain anonymous of course).

- Ensure that participants get some feedback on the final report.

- Never just assume that "it will be all right" - always seek permission or clarification before you access any information which you may think relevant (e.g. if you have documents on loan, never photocopy them without prior permission).

- Use your supervisor to bounce ideas off and to check your progress.

Optional Activity

Visit the companion website
            www.etextbooks.ac.uk/dissertation
to view more resources.

Background Reading

Blaxter, L., Hughes, C., and Tight, M. (2010) How to research (4th Edition). The Open University Press – Chapters 4 and 6

Bryman, A. (2012) Social Research Methods (4th Edition) Oxford University Press - Chapter 4

Hart, C. (1998) Doing a Literature Review: Releasing the Social Science Research Imagination. Sage Publications

6 METHODS OF RESEARCH

Objectives

To obtain consider a variety of possible research methods and relate this to the variety and style of the anticipated outcomes

Key Points

There are several different methods which may be pursued (or combined). These vary according to the nature of the subject being researched, (e.g. experimental chemistry or a social science opinion poll), the data being collected (text, numbers, tape recordings etc.), as well as the purpose – the research question or the hypothesis being tested in the research project.

There are a number of different research methods – systematic data gathering and structured techniques to enable critical investigation. The methods will differ with the nature of the subject being investigated, the duration of the project, and many other factors, including the motivations of the researchers. Some research projects may use overlapping methodologies of case studies to make sense of complex data.

Four main types of research method include: experimentation; survey; comparative study; and participant observation. Each have their strong and weak points. Each methodology requires the careful selection of variables and reactions to measure. In addition, experimental techniques usually require a control sample for comparison; survey methods are best developed from a pilot that can be used to test questions and data; and comparative study, though used in both primary and secondary research, needs to be carefully screened in order to make meaningful comparisons.

The selection of an appropriate research methodology for each project is a key initial decision which is closely related to the research question, and to the availability or accessibility of data. The ways in which you decide to select and measure that data may also be critical for your eventual presentation and the interpretation of the results, for example questionnaires may give us lots of empirical data, while focus groups might give us qualitative reactions and key areas for future investigation.

Even apparently simple techniques, such as watching, listening, reading, and structured interviews, can yield masses of complex data which needs to be carefully analysed in order to synthesise, correctly interpret, and understand the results. Research does not need to be complex in order to be useful or important. It is important to have sound and repeatable methods of measuring results, either on absolute or relative scales, and using fixed points or open-ended choice of questions. Some researchers may use an approach called Participatory Research to explore a wider and more meaningful involvement of the public in research activities.

In choosing research methods, the prime consideration should be based on what you want to find out. A secondary consideration relates to the skills, preferences, and biases which you will bring to the research project - how will this affect your results? Another important point is to consider what is (un)acceptable in the pursuit of your research, and the specific limitations of your chosen research methods. You may also want to consider the methods used by other researchers in relation to your area or topic of interest, and how effective or successful they have been. Finally, you should allow for the use of more than one research method in your studies, and include the flexibility to change direction if it appears that your research is running out of steam and/or skewing off at a tangent to what you consider to be the main issue(s). Triangulation (using different methods to interrogate the same subject area from different directions) will help you to test if your answers/responses are accurate and reliable, or perhaps just dependant on how you ask the question.

A key consideration in your choice of research methodology (the combined methods that you will use for evidence-gathering) will be the decision to choose a quantitative style (i.e. measuring data) or a qualitative style (assessing the relative value of data) or indeed a mixed method style (including both). You might care to consult Cresswell (2009) or Bryman (2008) for more information, and you should certainly discuss your options with your personal dissertation supervisor at this point.

Optional Activity

Read the relevant chapters given below. Write a couple of paragraphs in your research journal on what your initial choice of research methods might be, and explain why you have made this choice.

Setting the research question

Probably the first stage in your research project (whatever scale it is to be) is establishing your research question. This is important, because unless you know specifically what you are looking for, how will you know when you find it? Obviously there will be big research ideas, such as "How do we cure the common cold?" but in practice these are almost always broken down into a large number of small, more specific projects which, taken together, will hopefully make a positive contribution towards the eventual solution.

So, to start with, we need to identify the area of research interest. We can do this very generally at first, such as "My research area is about the experiences of people engaging in online education." This gives us a ball-park to start from and to begin to read the literature to narrow our field of enquiry.

The next stage will be to select a specific aspect of the research area – such as the use of the Managed Learning Environment, or perhaps a thematic issue such as "What are the undergraduate student experiences of learning science online?" This narrows the field of enquiry substantially and makes the literature search much more focused and more manageable.

From this more focused area of interest we can begin to ask a number of important questions, such as:

- What are the key aspects of online learning in science?

- Are some sciences easier to teach online?

- Is there a preferred model for mixing online tuition and practical sessions?

- What are the key elements of course design for online science classes?

To begin with you should write down all these questions as they occur to you. Some questions will be large and others, such as matters of definition, may be relatively easy to answer. When you have amassed a collection of questions (which you may continue adding to long after your dissertation has been handed in!), you should try to group the questions into the main key areas and roughly try to prioritise their importance.

In doing this exercise you will be able to select a major question that you wish to answer. It is important that the question is neither too general (or the project will be too vague) nor too specific (which might become exhausted in a very short space of time). It is also important that you treat this as a working title – which might evolve slightly over the life of your research. This allows you to begin to focus even more closely on the academic literature to determine what is already known about this specific research area and, importantly for your own new contribution to knowledge, what is less well-known.

Having established your working title, a good idea is to print a copy and stick it above your desk (or some other place that will catch your eye) because being reminded constantly of your prime research question will help to keep you on track and avoid interesting but time-consuming tangents in your work.

The use of a hypothesis

An alternative to the research question is to construct a hypothesis.

The Oxford Dictionary gives the definition of a

hypothesis as "a supposition or proposed explanation made on the basis of limited evidence as a starting point for further investigation".

Examples:

- All first year students are confused.

- All drugs are bad for your body.

- Sunday afternoons are always wet in Scotland.

- If I do X then Y will always result.

- Dogs do not eat fruit.

These are relatively simple statements which we have made. We do not as yet know if they are true, or false, or just occasionally true. In order to have confidence in these statements (or any other), we need to clarify the statements, (what are the students confused by? How 'wet' do we mean in millimetres of rainfall?)

We can then test the hypothesis. We do this by setting up a number of experiments which will prove, or disprove, the statement. These experiments may be simple or complex. They may be original, or draw upon the prior work of other researchers. They must, however, be repeatable, to give the same result(s).

It is possible to make conditional statements, such as:

- If the temperature is between 14 degrees C and 29 degrees C and the pressure is at 1 atmosphere, then mixture X will always be fluid.

We are setting conditions upon the truth of our statement. It is true, within certain defined limits. There is little point in saying that the statement is true 'sometimes' without being able to explain further when it is and when it is not true.

The hypothesis is a key element in many research projects. We are seeking to refine knowledge, and extend it from specific areas of known truths into more general rules which will enable us to predict and/or describe the phenomenon under investigation.

A hypothesis can be positive or negative, and when tested, a hypothesis might be refined, or split into several sub-statements. A hypothesis by itself proves nothing, but allows us to test its truthfulness, and in doing so it is a key tool in the research process.

Research questions or hypothesis?

Choosing between either a set of research questions or a hypothesis is an important stage in framing your research. It will also influence how you conduct your research in terms of your methods, the data collected, and how you analyse your findings.

How do you know when to choose between research questions or a hypothesis? This depends in part on the nature of your subject discipline, and in part on what you are interested in investigating. The nature of your subject discipline, and what you want to investigate, are important to establishing the 'research paradigm' or 'tradition' your work belongs within.

In very broad terms, many researchers make a distinction between 'positivism' and 'interpretivism' in terms of the two main 'research paradigms'.

Positivist research is viewed as objectivist in nature. This essentially means that it is characterised by a belief that the reality, phenomena or processes that we are interested in investigating can be directly measured through controlled experimentation that provides us with quantitative or quantifiable data. We then analyse the data collected to try and arrive at conclusions that are focused around what is true and untrue, or positive and false.

Interpretivist research is viewed as subjective and relativistic in nature. It is characterised by a belief that multiple interpretations or explanations are possible, and by the collection of qualitative data that will allow us to try and arrive at a reasonable and defensible set of findings and conclusions relating to the topic or phenomena under investigation.

Positivist research is most commonly associated with the physical sciences, for example maths, chemistry and physics. Because positivist research is concerned with objectivity, and quantifiable data that can lead to conclusions around what is true and untrue, or positive and false, it is more common to find hypotheses used to frame research in the physical sciences and related discipline areas. Interpretivist research is most commonly associated with the social sciences, and related areas, within which we want to understand and try to explain individual and collective experiences, social practices and phenomena, and the relationships between people and their environments. For this reason, it is more common to find research questions being used to frame research in social science based subjects, and for social science research to make more use of interviews, in-the-field observations, and written or recorded personal accounts of experience as the basis of data collection and analysis.

Identifying the 'research paradigm' or tradition that your discipline area belongs most closely to is a good starting point for making decisions about whether to use research questions or a hypothesis, the kinds of data you will collect, and the data analysis methods you will use. However, you should not let this constrain your approach. Be led by your supervisor in identifying whether research questions or a hypothesis are most appropriate to your own research project, and recognise that in practice many research projects in different discipline areas will often combine quantitative and qualitative approaches and methods.

The Use of Case Studies

Case studies use a combination of different methods to illustrate a particular problem, situation, or context by focusing on a small number of specific examples (even one!). Techniques such as interviews, document study, archive records et cetera may all be combined to use knowledge from different angles to describe a good (or bad) example, and to relate what actually happens in practice to a wider body of theory.

Advantages

- Ideally suited to small-scale research.

- Combine a number of study methods to give good detail.

- Can be used by other researchers to contrast, compare, and re-interpret.

- Usually show good 'down to earth' experiences.

- Allow attention to the subtlety and complexity of the particular case.

- Offer a good link to further action.

Disadvantages

- Care is needed in seeking to generalise from a limited sample area.

- Can sometimes be an excuse for just looking locally (e.g. your own workplace).

- Can be difficult and complex to organise and interpret data.

- Care needs to be taken to be analytical, not just descriptive.

Types of case study

In thinking about identifying and selecting appropriate case studies for your research project, it is worth being aware that there is an important distinction between knowing what case study research typically involves (as described above) and the different types of case study than can be undertaken. Stake (1994) differentiates between three main types of case study – intrinsic, instrumental, and collective – and provides a useful overview of what each involves.

An intrinsic case study is one undertaken in order to better understand a specific case object, whether that be an individual, an organisation, a social grouping or network, or a micro-level social context. In an intrinsic case study, the case itself is the main focus of the investigation (e.g. how a particular charitable organisation functions), rather than any generic social phenomena that can be seen to occur (e.g. how charitable organisations function). In an intrinsic case study, it is not expected that results will necessarily be applicable to other cases.

In an instrumental case study "a particular case is

examined to provide insight into an issue or refinement of theory" (ibid, p. 237). The case itself is of secondary interest, and it is chosen because it is expected to advance our understanding of a specific situation, social context, or phenomena (e.g. how new legislation helps or hinders establishing new charitable organisations, within which the nature of the charity itself is of secondary importance).

Collective case studies span multiple instrumental cases (two or more) across which there may be similarities and dissimilarities pertaining to the phenomena of interest, with each case chosen "because it is believed that understanding them will lead to better understanding, perhaps better theorizing, about a still larger collection of cases" (ibid, p. 237). A collective case study approach can be useful when no single case alone will allow all aspects of the chosen subject or phenomena to be explored, but where a combination of two or more cases will ensure that all the aspects that are of interest can be covered. An example here would be the use of social media to improve access to services for alcohol addiction. It may be that individual alcohol addiction groups only use one or two social media tools and platforms in their outreach work. However, looking at two different alcohol addiction groups as cases could allow the full range of social media tools of interest to be covered in the research.

Background Reading

Bell, J. (2010) Doing your research project: a guide for first-time researchers in education, health and social science (5th Edition). Open University Press.

Blaxter, L., Hughes, C., and Tight, M. (2010) How to research (4th Edition). The Open University Press - Chapter 3

Bryman, A. (2012) Social Research Methods (4th Edition) Oxford University Press. – Chapter 2 deals with research design, including case studies and Part Two of the book is devoted to a review of key research methods

Guba, E.G. & Lincoln, Y.S. (1994). Competing paradigms in qualitative research. In N.K. Denzin & Y.S. Lincoln (Eds.), Handbook of qualitative research methods (pp. 105-117). Thousand Oaks, California: Sage.

Stake, R.E. (1994). Case studies. In N.K. Denzin & Y.S. Lincoln (Eds.), Handbook of qualitative research methods (pp.236-247). Thousand Oaks, California: Sage.

7 COLLECTING INFORMATION

Objectives

To explore a variety of different techniques which can be utilised for the collection of data for the purposes of investigation, research and evaluation in your subject discipline.

Key Points

This focuses upon 6 main techniques of data collection - there are others, of course, and many can be used in combination, according to the needs of your investigations.

The main techniques are:

- literature review
- individual interviews
- focus groups
- observation
- questionnaires
- internet sources and other electronic retrieval.

Each of the above have their pros and cons, which are explored below.

We will also explore how you can engage with your wider research community, including online, as a means of keeping abreast of emerging research in your area, locating relevant resources, and beginning to publicise and even disseminating aspects of your research.

1. Literature review. All research to some extent consists of reading documents, reports, and/or journal articles which may shed a bearing on the nature of your project, often relating to similar projects in other areas and/or historical periods. Not all documents, however, have the same relevance nor importance in the research process. You should always check your sources. Do not use information which you cannot source or substantiate. The best research always traces the original primary research reports, rather than the secondary (or more) interpretation of these results by subsequent workers.

An important pre-cursor to conducting your literature review, and finding relevant journal articles and other documents, is to think about your search strategy. This involves making decisions about the library catalogues, search engines and bibliographic databases you will consult. Bibliographic databases (sometimes called citation indexes) are databases that carry extensive information about journal articles, monographs, reports, conference proceedings, books and book chapters, and often also patents. Academic libraries typically provide access to a good range of these, and many provide access to information about publications across multiple discipline areas (for example, Web of Science, which covers the sciences, social sciences, and arts and humanities). As well as making good use of academic library catalogues and bibliographic databases, your search strategy can also incorporate less formal routes to accessing relevant literature – for example, consulting with your supervisors and other more experienced colleagues to identify 'key literature' in the area of your research.

A critical element of any literature search strategy involves thinking about your search terms, in other words, the terms, words and phrases you will use to locate relevant information when using a library catalogue, bibliographic database or relevant internet search engines (for example, Google Scholar). It can be all too easy to use broad search terms that seem sensible, but which will result in a huge number of returns of varying quality and relevance.

As an example, imagine that you are interested in researching online learning. You could enter the following terms - online learning - into the search field of a library catalogue, database or search engine. This would return to you the details of any publications that lists the words online and learning, anywhere in the title, text or keywords of the publication. You could narrow this further by being specific about what you are interested in, and making use of quotation marks, parenthesis and something called Boolean search terms (the words AND, OR and NOT) to narrow your research. If you're specifically interested in the student experience of online learning, you could enter the following search terms – "online learning" AND "student experience". This would return details of any publications that feature the specific phrases "online learning" and "student experience" somewhere in the publication. This will return more precise results. However, you should also consider the fact that many authors and publications will use alternative words to refer to what you are interested in. For example, some papers will talk about 'online learning', but some will use alternative terms like 'online education' or 'blended learning'. Similarly some papers may make explicit reference to 'student experience' but some may instead use the words 'learners' and 'attitudes' or 'perceptions' to essentially talk about aspects of the student experience. In which case, you could construct something similar to the following – ("online learning" OR "online education" OR "blended learning") AND (student OR learner) AND (experience OR attitudes OR perceptions). It is possible to be even more precise than this, and to further refine your search strategy by using the 'advanced search' features of catalogues, databases and search engines. These features will allow you to narrow your search to specific time frames for publication (useful if you want locate only the most recent research), and also narrow your search to specific publication types (e.g. journal papers, books, patents etc.).

There are many good books and online resources on how to construct and conduct effective literature searches. The key point is to remember that what you get out of a literature search is often only as good as the search terms you put in and the sources of literature you consult.

2. Individual interviews These can be Structured (a pre-set list of questions) or Unstructured (allowing the interviewee to direct the conversation) or a mixture of both (Semi-structured). Each have their values, but can lead to a large amount of data which it is difficult to synthesise or draw an interpretation from. Advantages are that difficult subject areas such as attitudes and perceptions can be explored in a depth of quality which is impossible in simplistic 'tick-box' questionnaires. Objects, photographs et cetera can also be used to stimulate the interviewee, and can be a rich source of raising awareness of sensitive and/or difficult issues. Interviews can also be taped on audio or video and detailed transcriptions included as appendices, direct quotes, or case-study exemplars.

3. Focus groups This method of data collection may bring together a number of people to discuss particular topics in a structured or free-flowing manner. It is a useful technique to bring together a widely diverging range of expertise and/or opinion, but meetings need to be carefully planned, and must set ground rules for limiting discussion, dealing with conflict, and for encouraging creative and divergent thinking.

4. Observation Some types of research may be able to make use of the researcher as an observer, for example noting the reactions between participants, or the cause and effect of certain actions among the sample population. This can be a useful technique, but requires practice to identify bias of the researcher in the observation and interpretation of events (i.e. reporting strictly what is seen and not what is thought to be happening)

5. Questionnaires These are perhaps both the most common and the most confusing form of survey in research. They can be short or large, they can be directed at a small or a very large target population, and they can be very directive (i.e. tick a box from a pre-selected list of options) or completely open-ended (i.e. select your own issues and give your own reactions in your own words.) Great care needs to be taken in the construction in order to avoid ambiguity and/or irrelevant results - if there is more than one way to answer, someone will always choose the wrong way, perhaps spoiling your results. Always pilot your questionnaire before attempting your full survey. Be careful that you do not intimidate people by asking too much, or making it difficult to return questionnaires et cetera. A lot of data is good, but too much can kill a good project. It may be necessary to select a sample population and to extrapolate the results.

6. Internet Sources This can be a fast and effective way of gathering up-to-date information. The use of the World Wide Web, social networking, and e-mail applications is growing daily at a phenomenal rate. In many cases the internet offers high quality information which is not yet (or never will be!) in printed form. It is also easier and faster to update than the printed versions, but be warned, that not everything on the net is of the same standard, any more than you would expect to find all books or magazines equally truthful, comprehensive, or useful.

Engaging with your research community

When thinking about collecting information relevant to your research, be mindful to consider how you can tap into and draw upon the wider subject communities and research networks that you belong to – and realise that you do belong to such wider communities!

What might this mean in practice? Well, as alluded to previously, your research project supervisor is one such person in your wider community that you can turn to for advice and guidance on conducting your research and sourcing relevant information. However, there will also be other academics in your department, faculty or institution who will be knowledgeable about and engaged in research in your area of interest. Finding opportunities to talk to them can be invaluable, and your supervisor can help you in identifying relevant individuals.

Consider also making connections with more experienced peers, for example Masters or PhD students who are at a further stage of research in your area and who may be willing to share their experience and insights. PhD students are engaged in new, often cutting-edge research (more so than academic staff sometimes) and so are an invaluable source of current information. Academics and postgraduate students will also often be found presenting their work at internal departmental research seminars, or faculty conferences and events, so look out for opportunities like this and find out whether it is possible for you to attend.

You should also consider how you can make good use of online tools and communities to keep up to date with news and developments in your area of research. Within any discipline, you will find many emerging and established researchers sharing news and links to their latest work via Twitter and LinkedIn. Twitter can be used to follow leading researchers in your field. It is also often used for real-time themed chats amongst groups of like-minded researchers and academics, who gather online at pre-arranged times to discuss and share research and the latest developments in their field. Similarly you will almost certainly be able to find relevant discipline and research-related groups in your area of interest on LinkedIn. You may want to look for and join one or two such groups, follow the discussions, and potentially post requests and questions related to your research to the group.

There are also online mailing lists in many subject discipline areas that are worth joining in order to receive information and updates relevant to your research, and which you can also use to participate in discussion with other members of the list.

A good place to start in finding relevant mailing lists in your own area of research is to search though the mailing lists available at JISCMail, which maintains e-mail discussion lists for education and research communities based in the UK https://www.jiscmail.ac.uk

Finally, you may want to think about how you can use online tools and social media to disseminate your own research. Many students, particularly at more advanced levels of study (e.g. Masters and PhD level), maintain their own blogs to document and share their progress in their research projects with their supervisor and often a wider audience. If you are keeping an open online record of your project then be mindful of the distinction between sharing your general progress and not sharing anything of a confidential nature. As a matter of good practice always discuss the potential use of a project blog, or other online social media and networking tools, with your research project supervisor first.

Optional Activity

Visit the companion website
        www.etextbooks.ac.uk/dissertation
to view more resources.

You will probably want to use a combination of methods to gather information for your project. This is a good idea, but you will need to be sure that each method is chosen carefully and contributes something useful to your project. From your reading and other course activities you should try to identify the methods that you initially want to use to gather information for your dissertation (your ideas and methods may change as you read more and your project develops). In your research journal, write no more than three paragraphs (500-600 words) about your choice of research methods, why you have chosen them, and how they will significantly contribute to your task of gathering relevant information for your dissertation.

Background Reading

Blaxter, L., Hughes, C., and Tight, M. (2010) How to research (4th Edition). The Open University Press - Chapter 6

Bryman, A. (2012) Social Research Methods (4th Edition) Oxford University Press. – Part Two of the book is devoted to a review of key research methods

Hart, C. (1998) Doing a Literature Review: Releasing the Social Science Research Imagination. Sage Publications.

Ritchie, J. and Lewis, J. (Eds.) (2013). Qualitative research practice: a guide for social science students and researchers. Sage.

Shaw, M.D. (2007) Mastering online research: a comprehensive guide to effective and efficient search strategies. Ohio: F+W Publications.

FRANK RENNIE & KEITH SMYTH

8 THE PILOT PROJECT

Objectives

To appreciate the significance of running a formal pilot phase of a research project before commencing to collect the main data for analysis.

Key points

There are sound reasons why you should plan to try out your research techniques and methods before you embark seriously on gathering data for your project. These include:

- testing out how well your ideas work in practice

- sorting out the more useful (and unambiguous) questions which you want to ask

- checking the reality of gaining access to possible information

- getting some feedback on your ideas

- revising and modifying your plans on the basis of experience.

It is in the nature of a research project that things often do not work out as originally planned. Situations alter, people change jobs and opinions, the political climate shifts, or new information is uncovered, so even fairly simple projects can end up with results which you did not initially expect. The pilot phase is designed to uncover some of these pitfalls before you go too far down the road of collecting data which might end up being of little real use.

You will already have some experience of an informal pilot from the initial planning stage of your research project. At this time you will have spoken to a number of people about the possible direction(s) of your project, you may have interviewed a couple of key individuals in order to help form your ideas, and you may even have persuaded a couple of friends to complete draft versions of a questionnaire for you. All of these activities have, in a small way, helped you to test your ideas. This is the benefit of the pilot.

Now is the time to try an experiment to test your ideas. You should plan to sample a little bit of your chosen method(s) of data collection, whether this is by interview, questionnaire, document study, or participant observation. (You want a good sample, but do not be too ambitious - this is only a guide - save your big effort for the main project.) Try to complete a small number of interviews or questionnaires as if they are 'the real thing'.

You should make it clear to your participants that this is your pilot study (so that they know they can be constructively critical and also that another, more complete interview session will follow).

Now examine your results. You should work on the basis that if there is a way of getting the responses confused, then someone will do so! This is your opportunity to weed out the repetitive questions, or focus more clearly upon the key questions which you want to answer. Your questions should be clear and unambiguous, with a full range of options for response (e.g. $1 = $ Yes; $2 = $ No; $3 = $ Don't know).

Remember, you might not be able to explain your thoughts directly to your proposed participants, (especially with questionnaires) so the information which you give them must be clear and able to speak for itself.

If you discover that people in your pilot were getting confused with the wording of your question, or that some people have produced categories of response which you have not previously thought about, then this gives you the perfect opportunity to change your techniques. You can then be reassured that your methods will work well in your full survey.

A strong point in favour of running a pilot is that it gives you a chance to really sharpen up your key questions and get to grips with your subject in detail. Another advantage of the pilot is that it gives you some insight into the amount of time which is required for research work (always more than you initially thought!) so you can also gain a better idea if your project time scales and deadlines are realistic or if you should try to reduce the scale of your project at this stage.

The idea of a pilot is that it should be a learning experience which helps you make your full study stronger. There is no shame in admitting that you need to re-think your ideas, indeed it is better by far that you find that out at this stage before wasting precious time and money, so that you can improve your final version.

Optional Activity

Visit the companion website
        www.etextbooks.ac.uk/dissertation
to view more resources.

Consider how a pilot project might benefit your long-term project. Not all pilot projects take the same format, and not every major project needs a pilot, but there are certain undeniable benefits. For your particular project, try to list in two columns the advantages and disadvantages of running a pilot project. From these lists you should try to identify the exact way in which you will run a pilot project to help you improve your data collection for your main dissertation. If you decide not to run a pilot project in this instance, don't think that you are off the hook, because you will need to explain why not, and give some details on what other way you intend to test the robustness of your data gathering methodology.

Background Reading

Blaxter, L., Hughes, C., and Tight, M. (2010) How to research (4th Edition). The Open University Press - Chapter 5

Bryman, A. (2012) Social Research Methods (4th Edition) Oxford University Press. – See the sections that deal with piloting and pre-testing.

9 ANALYSIS OF THE DATA

Objectives

The objective is to introduce priorities for your consideration during the examination of the detailed components of the information which you will collect during your research project.

Key points

The analysis of your data is one of the pivotal points of your entire project. Regardless of whether the information which you have collected is wholly original and intellectually scintillating, or (hopefully not!) messy and full of failed ideas leading up blind alleys. This is the time at which you try to make a critical analysis to explain it all!

We use the term 'analysis' to mean a detailed examination of the facts (which you have gathered together). We will subsequently go on to interpret the meaning of these facts and statistics, and place them in a relevant context, but first we need to agree what the information is actually telling us. For this reason, even bad data can be better than none, so long as we can reasonably explain why it is bad, what went wrong, and how we can correct this in the future.

There are lots of different ways in which data can be analysed, and you might combine a number of different approaches in order to try to make sense of the mass of information which you have gathered from different sources.

Here are some key points to have in mind as you read through your data:

- How reliable is the data? (does it tell me what I wanted to know?).

- What are the gaps? (and are they important for this study?).

- What data can I do without? (is there anything which is not relevant - as opposed to anything which does not neatly fit your ideas?).

- What definitions and assumptions do I need to make clear? (so that others can understand my results).

- How can I reduce the mass of information to a useful summary? (without making it simplistic).

- Can I combine my information to shed new light on the subject? (i.e. comparing your new study with previously published results on a similar topic).

- Does the data give me a clear and consistent picture? (or does it simply show up all the other areas in which you are lacking detailed information?).

The analysis is basically a sorting process, and this process will differ according to the nature, style, and amount of the information which you have gathered. Your approach to how you look at documentary evidence will be different, for instance, to that of how you use information from interviews, or data which you have gained from questionnaires.

A reliable system of gathering, recording, and storing data is crucial to the process of analysing research information. You will now be reaping the rewards of your careful planning, preparation, and pilot study (or suffering from your lack of attention to detail!) The good news is that most research is a cyclic process, with the researcher(s) constantly testing the evidence, refining the research question(s) or hypothesis, and extending the boundaries of the investigations with further reading, interviews, experimentation, and/or questionnaires. The main thing is that you should learn from this process, and in terms of your dissertation, (or report) that you demonstrate what you have learned by explaining these stages of the investigation to your reader.

The key aims of your analysis are to make an assessment of your data in terms of:

- its reliability

- its significance

- its relevance

- its ability to be applied to a general situation beyond the confines of your own study.

You may also want to assess the usefulness of your data - though this is a relative term, that is to say, "usefulness to whom?"

Remember, data which does not comfortably fit into your

'ideal' pattern may not be due to any 'mistakes' by you, but might either be rogue data (e.g. questioning someone on a bad day!) or simply an exception to the 'rule'. Either way, this is important data and should not be ignored. We can often learn just as much from the 'exceptions' as we can from the mainstream data which conveniently fits our predictions.

Optional Activity

Draw a three column table. In the first column insert all the different types of information that you will need to complete your project (e.g. "Information on what people think about X" or "data to compare village Y with other villages". In the second column write how you will gather this information (e.g. it might be 'Structured interviews' and 'reading academic literature'. In the third column you should insert how you intend to analyse this data (e.g. it might be "create a matrix of responses against the types of people questioned" and "compare 10 key characteristics between selected villages".

A good way to help you structure and classify the types of data that you will require is to maintain a list of questions in your research journal. Jot down the questions as they occur to you – some will be easy to answer, others almost impossible – but when you group this long list together in clusters of similarity you may find some promising areas for further definition and investigation.

Background Reading

Blaxter, L., Hughes, C., and Tight, M. (2010) How to research (4th Edition). The Open University Press - Chapter 7

Bryman, A.(2012) Social Research Methods (4th Edition)

Oxford University Press – Part Three deals with a variety of analytical methods for research projects

Ritchie, J. and Lewis, J. (Eds.) (2013). Qualitative research practice: a guide for social science students and researchers. Sage.

10 STRUCTURING RESEARCH

Objectives

To gain an appreciation of the importance of careful planning in the design structure and monitoring of an investigative project.

Key Points

In addition to planning the critical tasks and setting deadlines for investigative projects, it is important to understand the specific structure of the project. This may be broken down into 8 general categories:

- an introduction to the theme and the specific background to the research or (including its relevance)

- a summary of the current state of knowledge of this subject area – gained mostly from academic literature and other reputable sources (this is your literature review)

- details (and relevance) of the method(s) of investigation to be employed (your methodology)

- specific results from the study

- analysis, interpretation and discussion of the results

- conclusions [and/or answers to the research question(s)]

- references and bibliography

- any appendices required to support the evidence in the body of the report.

These categories may be condensed or subdivided, according to the nature of the study, and the reporting procedure may be written (i.e. a dissertation) or other media (e.g. a video documentary). The whole process, however, needs to be considered in order to present a comprehensive analysis of the investigation. There is no implication that these categories should have the same rank in importance or depth of detail - this will depend heavily upon the individual project and the individual researcher.

The structuring of an investigative project requires more than simply mapping the possible headlines and setting some time limits - though both of these are important - it also requires a number of practical activities which will assist the smooth management of the investigative project.

Such activities include the piloting of research methods and/or systems of gathering information. This involves testing your methodology (e.g. questionnaire or interview technique) on a small number of information sources (people and/or organisations) which are similar to your eventual target population. It is important that this pilot is undertaken rigorously and honestly, otherwise it is not worth doing. It is designed to spot flaws and errors in your method which can be corrected at an early stage before your project moves to a larger audience.

Also important is the ability to rethink elements of your investigative project, and if necessary to redesign the elements (e.g. research questions, data collection, target population etc.) if things are starting to go wrong (or not go at all!). In this, you should not be afraid to seek the advice of a supervisor or research colleague, but also it is important to manage your own project and move it forward without (or despite!) external direction.

Further specific guidance on how to organise and undertake the writing up of your research project is provided in Chapter 14 The research report.

Optional Activity

Visit the companion website
                www.etextbooks.ac.uk/dissertation
to view more resources.

Construct a simple Gantt chart to enable you to structure your research work effectively. This need not be overly elaborate, but you should include an accurate time line across the top of your chart, and a detailed list of realistic tasks and activities that require completion down the left-hand column. Indicate the duration and importance of the tasks. This is not a cosmetic exercise, and you will find that you need to refer to this at several stages during your research in order to meet your deadlines effectively.

There are a number of useful, free, web-based tools that you can utilise to assist your planning – for example in the construction of Gantt charts, arranging meetings, sharing academic articles, organising references, work-flow planning, and setting alerts to notify the publication of new resources – and some of these are listed on the companion website at URL:

Background Reading

Blaxter, L., Hughes, C., and Tight, M. (2010) How to research (4th Edition). The Open University Press - Chapter 5

Bryman, A. (2012) Social Research Methods (4th Edition) Oxford University Press – See the sections that deal with a variety of methods for structuring research projects

11 ORGANISATING RESEARCH RESULTS

Objectives

To understand the importance of adopting practical and relevant methods for the organisation of research results to enable analysis.

Key Points

It is important to recognise from the start that you should collect and analyse your information in a logical and consistent manner. It is also important to realise that you do not need to wait until all of the information is collected before you begin to analyse it.

In preparing the pilot study of your chosen investigative technique (survey etc.), you need to consider the implications of the sample size, how representative your sample population is compared to the population at large, your style of sampling (random versus structured) and the effect of sampling in different geographical areas.

It may become apparent at a relatively early stage of your study that you need to extend or contract your study due to too little or too much information. It may also be that your sample is skewed in certain ways which will bias your results (e.g. asking a question about the desirability of alcohol and only sampling the participants at a temperance meeting!). Early analysis of your results may help to identify accidental biases and limitations of your technique(s) and help you correct them before you get too far into your study.

If you are engaged in comparative studies, then it is important to achieve a consistency of method(s) to allow truthful comparison and to minimise systematic errors. In any experiment, it is always best to change one variable at a time, then observe the results. To change two or more variables at the one time will lead to uncertainty as to precisely which variable is causing the observed result. In comparative studies, the importance of time and place can be crucial. It may be possible for you to replicate studies which have been carried out by others at a different location (region/country) or different time (months/years earlier). Depending on the nature of your study, it may also be possible for you to replicate your own study (in a different time or place) and in doing so add a richness to the quality of your data.

The process of organising the raw results from surveys et cetera can be a long, complicated, and exhausting business. It is made easier if you can prepare a standard format or 'coding' through which you can assemble and present the data easily. In broad terms, 'coding' is the process by which we systematically categorise the data we have collected in order for it to be analysed and presented. Our approach to coding data is very much dependent on the methods of data collection we have used, and for example surveys, interviews, field observation, and content analysis of documents all have their own coding conventions.

There are a number of statistical packages available for quantitative forms of analysis, for example SPSS (Statistical Package for the Social Sciences), and for analysis of qualitative interview data. However, even hand-drawn or annotated electronic data files which are coded to summarise your results will be invaluable if you should choose to illustrate your analysis with graphs, tables, and cross-tabulated diagrams (comparing how one factor varies with the variability of another).

It is a vital step in the organisation of your data to design your questionnaires or surveys to make the eventual coding process easier. You should use the results of your pilot sample to prepare coding guides and to think about the types of diagrams which you might want to use eventually. This will allow you to redesign the questionnaire and to make the most efficient use of the data sets which your survey might produce.

Optional Activity

Visit the companion website
        www.etextbooks.ac.uk/dissertation
to view more resources.

Look at your study methodology and the results of your pilot study (this need only be 3 or 4 questionnaires / interviews). How do you intend to code your study to give clear and unambiguous results? What did you learn about coding from your pilot study? Do you intend to use Excel or some other form of spreadsheet to collate and display your results? Will this allow you to analyse the results, produce graphs, or otherwise present your collected results graphically?

Write notes for yourself on your experience of coding so far and any helpful lessons that you have learned.

Background Reading

Blaxter, L., Hughes, C., and Tight, M. (2010) How to research (4th Edition). The Open University Press – Chapters 6 and 7

Bryman, A. (2012) Social Research Methods (4th Edition) Oxford University Press – Part Four deals with the organisation of research projects

12 STATISTICS IN RESEARCH

Objectives

To gain a practical appreciation of the use and importance of statistical information in the presentation and interpretation of research results.

Key Points

There are three golden rules:

1) never use statistics which you personally don't understand and cannot explain to others

2) keep statistics as simple as possible (so that others can fully understand what you mean)

3) ensure that any statistics used are relevant to the points you want to convey.

It is almost a truism that 'statistics can be used to prove anything' but the art of statistics is to know how to use figures to express clearly what you want to say about your data and/or results. You should always use statistics circumspectly, for, unless you know the real significance of the statistics which you are using, there is a very real danger that they will be meaningless (at best) or misleading (at worst). Even apparently simple calculations, such as limits of error, or a simple comparison between two populations (chi-squared test), can be very misleading if insufficient or inadequate data is used to begin with.

Correctly used statistics can be used to verify the accuracy of your assumptions (e.g. by comparing variations from a norm) or to compare the similarity or difference between two sets of data (e.g. comparing the responses of men and women to the same set of questions). More simply, the response rate to certain questions and situations can be expressed as a percentage of the respondents (e.g. "50% of those sampled said...."). In more sophisticated analyses, the varying strength of opinion to certain options can be expressed on a sliding scale (e.g. from 1 to 10) which may suit very well for comparative analysis, or for correlation with other variables (such as the differences in strength of opinion between different regions, or different times, or different groups of people.)

Another important statistical test allows us to establish the extent of the correlation between two variables. The correlation is said to be positive if one factor increases as the other factor increases (e.g. the height of children generally increases with increasing age) or negative if one factor decreases as another increases (e.g. manual dexterity of co-ordination decreases with increasing alcohol consumed). It is important to realise that the existence of a good correlation does not necessarily indicate a cause and effect relationship. Statistics may be used to calculate the probability of an outcome, and may therefore be used to model or predict likely outcomes, which can be experimentally tested in real life.

These relationships may be expressed as simple statistics, or summarised in appropriate tables, or translated to appropriate graphs and/or diagrams.

Descriptive versus inferential statistics

When approaching the use of statistics in your research, it is worth being mindful of the distinction between descriptive and inferential statistics. Descriptive statistics are called 'descriptive' because they essentially help us summarise data in a clear way that will allow overall patterns to be seen. Frequency and percentage counts (e.g. the number or percentage of values, respondents or responses that fall into a particular category) are a basic form of descriptive statistics. Tables, bar and pie charts are all common ways of presenting such data. Mean (average value e.g. average age), mode (most frequently occurring value e.g. most common age) and median (the middle value in a numerically ordered range of values e.g. the age at the mid-point in a series of respondents' ages) are also common descriptive statistics.

While descriptive statistics help us to identify trends and patterns, and present data succinctly in tabular or visual forms, they do not allow us to draw concrete conclusions regarding the relationships between different variables or factors.

Inferential statistics are more complex. They allow us to look at the relationship between different variables, to test hypotheses, and to draw conclusions about our sample population that we might infer can also apply to the wider population from which the sample was drawn. The correlation examples provided above are examples of inferential statistics.

Why is it important to know about the distinction between descriptive and inferential statistics? It is important in understanding and interpreting statistical data in the literature you may be reviewing for your research, but also in making decisions about the kinds of statistical analysis you may want to conduct and present for your own research. Research that is primarily qualitative in nature is less likely to make use of inferential statistics, although it may use descriptive statistics in presenting the findings from a questionnaire used to complement interviews, or in presenting basic demographic information about the group of subjects involved in the research. Conversely, research that is primarily quantitative and experimental in nature is more likely to use inferential statistics to look at the relationships between variables (e.g. age and height) and to try and prove or disprove a hypothesis.

Optional Activity

Visit the companion website
            www.etextbooks.ac.uk/dissertation
to view more resources.

Background Reading

Blaxter, L., Hughes, C., and Tight, M. (2010) How to research (4th Edition). The Open University Press - Chapter 7

Bryman, A.(2012) Social Research Methods (4th Edition) Oxford University Press – Chapters 12 to 14 cover aspects of the use of statistics in research

13 GRAPHICS IN RESEARCH

Objectives

The main aim is to illustrate a range of different methods for the graphical presentation of research results which can assist with the interpretation and understanding of complex information.

Key Points

The emphasis of all graphics, diagrams, maps et cetera which are used to illustrate project dissertations and research results should be on simplicity of the figures, relevance to the accompanying text, and clarity of understanding. It is much better to have a series of clear, simple diagrams which can help the reader to understand your results and/or interpretation(s) than to have a more complex (cluttered) diagram which might look more impressive, but which only serves to confuse the reader.

There are a number of statistical computer packages on the market which will produce a wide range of diagrams from a database or spreadsheet designed to your own specifications. These packages are generally very effective in the right hands, but you must know what you are trying to achieve with your diagrams, and really understand what is being expressed. Diagrams can be hand drawn if you prefer, and though they should be neat, the emphasis, again, should be on clarity rather than creating a great work of art. The explanation and the interpretation are much more important than spending hours trying to achieve a 'perfect' diagram. Comparison of your study with previous studies may be a bonus.

It is important to select the appropriate diagrams to maximise the impact of the point(s) which you are trying to establish, and you should always have your potential readership in mind. It may be, for instance, that you want to include a map of your sample area, but there may be little point in only illustrating your village in great detail if your reader is unaware of the country and/or region where your village is situated. It may be important to include insert maps and keys which help to place the geographical location of your subsequent, more detailed, maps.

In a similar manner, you should experiment with several different styles of graphics which can show different ways of representing the same information. They will all have different strengths and weaknesses. A simple pie-chart can show the relative importance of different sectors of your population, though this may also be represented by a histogram, a simple line-graph or a bar-chart. It may be appropriate to plot a large number of data points on a scatter diagram on which you attempt to identify clusters and trends) or you may choose to use a stack-chart which will allow the comparison of additional variables.

There are many different types of useful diagrams, but the greatest priority is to combine your data in such a way as to give you the detail of individual results, while allowing a comparison of the broad trends and the identification of general models or patterns.

If you use diagrams and/or maps from other locations you must cite the source of your diagrams. This is particularly relevant for copyright diagrams, but in general, every source that you copy from should be acknowledged fully. You may find it useful to search for Creative Commons resources, and you can do this on, for example, Flickr and Google Images simply by clicking the 'advanced search' button and specifying the you want to search for Creative Commons materials. These materials also have restrictions on their use, but normally they have been approved for reuse for educational purposes provided that you fully acknowledge the creator of the resource and the location (web address) where you found the material. Click on the link to 'license' to confirm the conditions of reuse.

A Pie Chart Display

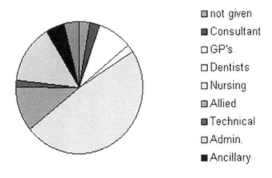

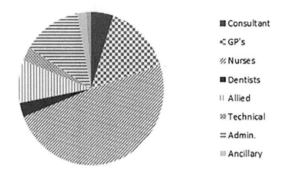

The pie chart diagram above shows a simple graphical way to express the relative proportions of different sectors of a sample population. The value of each sector is calculated as a fraction of the total population value and is then multiplied by 360 degrees to give the area of a circle which this sector would cover. It is a simple and effective way of illustrating some results, and some software packages allow sectors to be pulled out of the circle in order to emphasise their importance. Notice the different effects between colour and black-and-white print – be sure to make your categories easily readable.

A Histogram Display

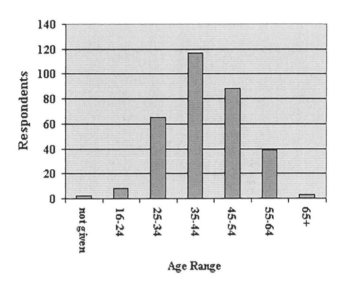

Age Range of Respondents

The histogram is a very simple form of graphical display which enables easy comparison of numerical data. The researcher is required to set the number and range of sub-divisions for the data, usually regular divisions, but not always so. The diagram above displays the age range of the number of people who replied to a research study. The display gives no extra detail, such as where the replies came from, nor about the gender of the respondents. An advantage of this graph is that it presents easy to understand information. To include a more complex range of information, you might choose to add other simple histograms, or select a more complex type of graph.

A Line Graph Display

Average temperatures for Tiree 1951-80

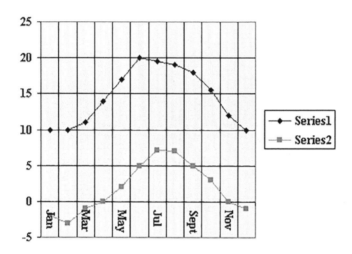

   The simple line chart plots the change of one variable against another. In the chart above the maximum and minimum temperatures for the island of Tiree are given for a specific period of time. Notice that there is a clear relationship between the two lines plotted, both min. and max. temperatures were higher in summer than in winter. It is a useful device to compare with information from other sites, for example a superimposed plot of the temperatures for a New Zealand town would give the opposite curve due to seasonal differences.

A Scatter Diagram Display

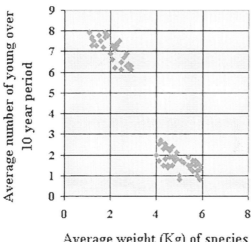

Relationship between birth rate and weight

This scatter diagram can be used to illustrate that the experimental results cluster clearly around two distinct groups. The population of Species X with an average weight at birth of greater than 4kg is likely to produce a clutch size of three or less individuals, whereas those with an average weight of less than 3kg at birth are likely to be in clutches of greater than 6 young. This is useful for identifying distinct groups (and also possibly a sliding scale between groups) but it does not explain why there is such a difference. To know that this difference exists, however, is very useful, and we can then devise different theories to test potential reasons for it.

A Stack Chart Display

Occupations by location

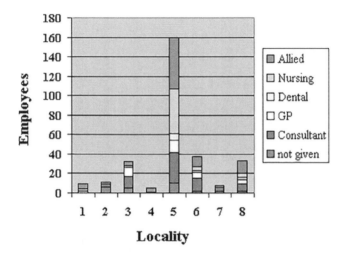

The stack chart is a type of histogram which enables complex comparison between variables in order to illustrate how certain attributes of a variable may change, even within the same variable category. For instance, in the diagram above, it is clear than not only is there a difference in employment types between different locations, but also there is a very big difference in the total numbers of people employed at each location. These diagrams can be very useful for displaying the changing patterns of multiple variables, but just be careful not to get too ambitious. A cluttered diagram makes it difficult to interpret, and this leads to a loss of understanding.

A Straight Correlation Display

Link between disturbance and feeding of young

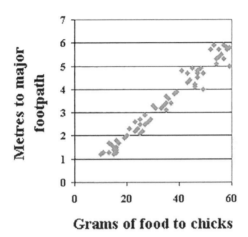

Grams of food to chicks

In the above diagram there is a direct relationship between one factor and another. In this case it is the link between the closeness of the young chicks to a major footpath and the amount of food which these chicks receive. We can use this to test for potential solutions to this correlation, for example the level of disturbance on the footpath may prevent the parents from returning to the nest site as frequently in comparison to more remote sites. This, however, we can only guess at and try to test by experiment. Our graph does not tell us why there is a correlation, only that there is one (and this can be a positive or a negative link). We can use the line of best fit to try to predict the values we do not know, then compare this with the reality to test if our predictions accurately model reality.

Background Reading

Blaxter, L., Hughes, C., and Tight, M. (2010) How to research (4th Edition). The Open University Press - Chapter 7

Bryman, A. (2012) Social Research Methods (4th Edition) Oxford University Press – Chapter 15 deals with aspects of the presentation of research data (although note that others statistical programmes are also available and broadly similar in what they offer).

14 THE RESEARCH REPORT

Objectives

To present some general principles which are necessary to consider when writing up research results (and how to make a difficult process as easy as possible.)

Key Points

The write-up of your investigative project is not merely the finishing touch of your research work, it is also an important purpose of the work itself. There is little point in seeking to contribute something new to human knowledge if you are unwilling or unable to share it with your colleagues and peers. This sharing needs to follow very careful rules in order to be clear, readable, interesting, and unambiguous. Publication is a sharing process.

It is never too early to make a start in writing-up your work. Obviously, there are major limitations when you first start off, but even at this stage you can begin to draft the general contents of your report (or dissertation). General headings can be revised and progressively refined as your research project takes shape – but a surprising amount can frequently remain quite flexible until a very late stage in your write-up. It is often possible to 'top-and-tail' your work, that is, to write an introductory section on the background to your chosen topic, and at the same time begin to compile a relevant bibliography or list of references which you have consulted in the preparation of your dissertation.

For large reports, you might like to negotiate with your supervisor for constructive comments on the draft of each chapter or the main section of your dissertation as you progress. With smaller projects this will not be necessary, but you might chose to seek comment on a final draft, before actual submission of your dissertation for examination.

It is important that you try to put your project, however small, into a wider context, by relating it to the published work of other researchers. In doing so you might want to explore certain key themes, and attempt to show how these link to the issues which you have investigated. It is bad form to rubbish the work of previous researchers - even if they did get it wildly wrong (according to you!) they will usually have done the best possible job under the restrictions and state of knowledge at that time. You should certainly critically appraise prior work, - not everything that gets published is true - but only to evaluate it in the light of its relationship with your own experiences, experiments, and/or background reading. Knowledge often progresses incrementally, and it is your task to move it on to a next stage by careful argument, revealing new facts, and an elegant interpretation of the information which is available to you at the time of writing. (You may revisit the subject years later, and with more knowledge, be embarrassed by the naiveté of your own conclusions!)

In this context it is also important to know when to stop writing. A real enthusiast will want to go on and on and on researching into their chosen subject - but it is critically important to be able to draw your information together and present conclusions - even if you then embark on a 'phase 2' of deeper and more extensive research on the same topic.

Optional Activity

Visit the companion website
                www.etextbooks.ac.uk/dissertation
to view more resources.

Background Reading

Blaxter, L., Hughes, C., and Tight, M. (2010) How to research (4th Edition). The Open University Press - Chapter 8

Bryman, A. (2012) Social Research Methods (4th Edition) Oxford University Press.

15 THE STRUCTURE OF THE DISSERTATION

What should my dissertation look like?

Each project dissertation will vary to some degree in the length of the individual chapters, but there is general agreement on what should be included in a good dissertation and the chronological order of the chapters as you progress through your investigation of the topic. You should use the following general structure, and discuss the details of the individual chapters with your Tutor.

1. Declaration

2. Abstract

3. Contents

4. Introduction and Literature review

5. Methodology

6. Results of the main topic(s)

7. Interpretation of the results and discussion

8. Conclusions and evaluation

9. Recommendations for further research (if

appropriate)

10. References

11. Appendices

How long is enough?

There is no 'standard' length for a dissertation – the number of words required, like the specific contents, depends entirely upon the subject nature of the research and the academic level of investigation. Normally, the description for the course of study will give an upper limit for the total word count, and it is important that these should be adhered to. A typical example would be 8,000-10,000 words for an undergraduate honours dissertation; around 15,000 words for a taught Masters degree; and up to 100,000 words for a doctoral dissertation – but this will vary. These upper limits are usually strictly observed, but there is no obligation to write to the maximum, some dissertations, such as mathematics and physics, may consist of far fewer words because they are based upon complex equations and calculations.

Similarly, there is no 'blueprint' for the length of each section or chapter, although as a rule-of-thumb the scene-setting (introduction and literature review) might be about one-quarter of the total word count; the methodology chapter perhaps slightly shorter and more succinct; with the remainder of the word-count being spread appropriately between the presentation of the results and the analysis/conclusions chapters. The total word count usually refers to the entire main text, including footnotes or endnotes (which should be kept to an absolute minimum, if they are used at all!) but does not include the abstract, the references, or the appendices. The appendices should only contain information that is essential to the main text, but which might clutter the main text if it were to be included there (e.g. large tables of numerical information, large lists of organisations consulted, or specific legal definitions that are relevant but supplementary to the explanation in the main text.)

While the basic structure of the dissertation is generic, the specific contents will vary with the subject discipline, and the expected contribution to scholarship will vary with the context and academic level of the subject being studied. It is considered acceptable, for instance, to include more descriptive writing to set the scene at the undergraduate level (provided it leads to an appropriate level of analysis) whereas at postgraduate level description should be kept to a minimum and backed-up by independent evidence from the academic literature. The focus at postgraduate level is very firmly on the robust design of the methodology and a detailed analysis of the results gathered. For a PhD, the main stipulation is that the dissertation should be a) all your own work, and b) an original contribution to knowledge in the subject area. At all postgraduate levels there is an expectation that students will consult the primary research sources and not refer to, or be reliant on, only secondary sources of literature.

The steps from Honours undergraduate to Taught postgraduate to Doctorate could be summarised as follows. While it is expected at all three levels that the work presented is the student's own work, the levels of analysis and originality (in the research topic and/or methods) would be expected to increase with advancing academic level. It is also expected that the students will take greater control over their own research process, and become more self-directed, as they progress from undergraduate to Doctorate. The distinction between a Masters by research and a Doctorate is that while the Masters dissertation could provide an answer to a specific problem or location (e.g. a particular engineering problem or an analysis of a certain Local Authority region) the Doctorate would expect this plus an explicit explanation on how the results/conclusions contribute to a better understanding of the subject discipline as a whole. In other words, the Doctoral dissertation is expected to place the specific research question in the wider context of the subject discipline and show how this knowledge contributes to an advancement of the discipline as a whole.

Declaration

Inside the front cover of your dissertation, before you come to anything else, you should insert a Declaration to affirm that the work which you are presenting has been undertaken by yourself as an original submission for your assessment in this degree programme.

The wording of this declaration should be as follows:

Declaration

This dissertation is submitted in partial fulfilment for the award of the degree of BSc in Sustainable Rural Development (Or other relevant degree title).

I certify that this is my own work.

Signed:

Date:

You should then sign and date the declaration in your own handwriting.

Do not include anything else on this page.

Abstract

As a mandatory requirement for your dissertation, the abstract is likely to be the shortest, yet the most difficult, piece that you will have to write. It is also likely to be one of the most useful sections. It is the first (and in many cases the only) part of your dissertation that people will read. People will frequently use the abstract to decide if it is worth reading more of your work - so it is important that you get the abstract right. Although the abstract is placed as the first section of your dissertation (before even the Contents page!) it is probably going to be the very last thing which you write on your study. The reason for this is that the abstract needs to be a self-contained summary of what you actually did – including a short explanation on what, why, and how the work was done, what you found out, and what the significance is for the subject area.

The function of the abstract is to summarise accurately but briefly (usually between 200 and 400 words maximum) the scope of your project.

You should include:

- the nature of your project (what it is about)
- its context (how it is placed within the wider subject area)
- how it was carried out (your methodology)
- a summary of your its major findings (your results and/or conclusions).

A good abstract is written in the present tense and will convey to your potential readership all of the key points covered in your dissertation, paper, or article.

An abstract compels authors to distil their words of wisdom into the most fundamental components, and for this reason the abstract is frequently written with the benefit of hindsight, as your final words on your work.

Before you attempt to write the abstract for your dissertation you should:

- check a number of relevant academic journals to get a feel for how experienced authors write their abstracts.

- select a book or other text which you have found useful and write an abstract using no more than 200 words. Check it with your Supervisor.

- check the abstracts of previous dissertations as a comparison with your own.

Contents

You should set out a clear list of the contents of the main parts of your work.

As a general guide, you should number the chapters and key sections/sub-section then indicate their page number in the main text. You may wish to list subsidiary headings using a slightly smaller font (e.g. point 14 for the main headings and point 12 for the subtext) and number these subheadings accordingly.

List the appendices in your main contents pages, but use a separate, subsequent page to itemise all your tables, graphs, maps, and other graphical illustrations which have included in the dissertation. Include details of their location in the text, say:

Graph 1 - Analysis of replies by rural sector. – either "page 23" or "between pages 34 and 35"

Do not try to cram as much as possible into the contents page - spread out your text over 2 or 3 pages if necessary.

The text below is a model of a contents page which you can adapt for use in your own work.

Example:

1.	**Background to the area**	**9**
2.	**Literature review of the subject**	**14**
3.	**Methodology**	**28**
4.	**Results**	**34**
	4.1, The public meetings	34
	4.2, The questionnaire	39
	4.3, The structured interviews	46
5.	**Interpretation of results**	**50**
	5.1, Analysis of local opinion	50
	5.2, Comparison with local agency plans	55
	5.3, Proposed activities for the area	58
6.	**Conclusions and recommendations**	**64**
7.	**References**	**70**
8.	**Appendices**	**81**

Introduction and Literature Review

This is the section in which you introduce the topic of your project in greater detail. To do this you need to be able to:

- explain what your topic is
- place it in a wider context for your studies

- demonstrate your familiarity with the background literature on this topic

- illustrate the general implications of your study for the subject as a whole.

You need to show that you have a knowledge and understanding of the most recent and/or relevant literature published in the academic journals and textbooks pertinent to your discipline. Do not simply accept the views of other authors uncritically, you are encouraged to challenge them and contrast them with the opinions of others. You do, however, need to provide evidence to substantiate your own comments and views.

The introduction needs to set the scene for your subsequent chapters, so you must build up the text logically from your initial general statement on your project (your working title) to a specific statement on what exactly you intend to investigate in subsequent chapters.

This is more than simply a literature review of your chosen topic, although this will form a major theme of your introduction. You will need to carefully explain the historical development of your subject area, so that the reader is able to understand your perspective on the current position which you are choosing to investigate.

It is likely that your reader (or examiner?) will have a general familiarity with your chosen subject area, so it is unnecessary to explain every last detail, but it is important that you give sufficient explanation to convince the reader (examiner) that you know what you are talking about!! This is especially true when you are introducing new and/or unfamiliar terms, technical concepts, or academic theories and interpretations.

Whether you are agreeing, challenging, or conceding an existing point of view, whether you are proposing a new idea or reformatting existing opinions, you must reference your text to the authors of the wider body of materials which have helped you to form your opinions.

Your introduction should aim to be self-explanatory, that is, it should not need any summary or appendix to succeed in giving a new reader a detailed and balanced 'taster' to the topic which you have selected.

Methodology

The methodology is the key to a good research project. It will make or break all other parts of your study, no matter if you are looking at a huge, expensive project, or a one-day snapshot profile of a topic.

As a consequence, you need to be clear, unambiguous, and precise about the methods of study which you select - and also about the reasons why you have rejected other methods.

The chapter in your dissertation in which you describe your methodology is at least (if not more) important that your final results. You need to reflect this in the length, clarity, and care which you take to write this section.

There are several basic points which you need to consider:

- What do you want to find out?

- Which different methods will you be able to use in your study?

- Which methods are likely to give you the sort of data which you are seeking?

- Can you justify your choice(s)?

- Which methods can you discard, and why?

- Will your choice of methods affect the answers you get?

- Is this acceptable?

- Should you use a combination of methods?

- What are the ethical dimensions of your choice?

You should include an explanation and discussion of all the above points in your chapter on methodology. It is important that your reader understands the techniques which you will be using, and why you have selected them. The selection of different methods will have a critical influence on the nature and quality of the information which you will be able to gather.

Too many corners cut, or too many ambiguous assumptions made at this stage will result in weak (or worthless) subsequent chapters discussing the results, interpretations, and conclusions.

It is therefore crucial at this stage to ensure that you devote sufficient thought to justify the methodology which you will adopt, and to make sure that you clearly document these choices in your dissertation, (with reference to the relevant academic literature and previous studies).

If it is appropriate, you might like to include an evaluation of your methods in your conclusions section, or include a section on further research opportunities which your study has uncovered but which you have been unable to pursue (through lack of time, resources, ability, etc.).

Results

In this section you should give a detailed report of the results that your study has produced.

Depending on the nature of your study (and after discussion your results with your supervisor) you have two main choices.

- To present the results in a straight, dry descriptive format, followed by a separate chapter dealing with the interpretation of these results

- To combine the presentation of the results with a commentary and interpretation as you go along, perhaps dealing with a more in-depth discussion and conclusions in a subsequent chapter.

Either way, this is the chapter where you give the details to your readers of what the results are of your research project. You will want to break this down into the separate elements of your methodology, for example as a separate sub-section on the results from the questionnaire survey, another sub-section for the results from the semi-structured interviews, perhaps another sub-section on the focus group results. Obviously this will depend upon which methodology you used.

Do not try to squash all your results together – list and describe the results produced in each of the sub-sections individually. There is a good reason for this. When you examine a situation from several different angles, using several different research methods, you can compare if you get similar or contradictory results from the different methods. This is called triangulation of the results, and when you get are able to obtain very similar results even when approaching the problem from different perspectives and using different research methods, it gives very strong evidence of the nature of reality. Whether you can fully or adequately explain this evidence is a very different issue!

If you decide to present your results in one chapter and then give a structured, in-depth interpretation in a following chapter, don't be too worried if the simple presentation of your results looks a bit dry. The main thing is that you are able to express your results clearly and accurately, without embellishment or the addition of wishful thinking, then at some point attempt to analyse, interpret, and explain what you think these results actually mean. It is important at this point to keep your initial research question (or hypothesis) firmly in mind. You need to consider what your results tell you that will help to answer the research question (or proves/disproves the hypothesis). Anything else might be very interesting, might even be worthy of further research, but it is spurious to your research question and therefore a distraction to you finishing your dissertation write-up.

Interpretation

In this section you are encouraged to speculate and draw lessons from your own results and the results of other studies which you have drawn upon during the pursuit of your own project.

It is important to recognise and make explicit your own position within your research project.

It is crucial to realise that you can disagree with previous researchers but you should be temperate in your criticism (they may not have had all the facts available to you) and also to substantiate your own views (otherwise others will criticise you in turn for your lack of proof, or for your misinterpretation of the detail).

Key points to consider are:

- you do not need to restate your results, but you will need to emphasise and explain the results

- you will need to consider alternative explanations

- you will need to put the results into a wider context of thematic and/or regional issues

- you will need to consider the value and quality of your results

- you will need to combine your results to describe and explain a coherent analysis - even if this means pointing out contradictions, anomalies, and sectors in which data is weak or missing.

Do not:

- stray from the topic

- let your imagination dominate over the evidence available to you

- be verbose - crisp, concise statements are by far the best treatment

- be too ambitious. It is better to complete a modest project well than to make a complete mess of a larger project

- become subjective - keep your distance and do not personalise your discussion - stick to the evidence which can reasonably be deduced from your own results and background reading.

Use this chapter to bring together the main strands

from the previous chapters - introduction, methods, and results - in order to provide a coherent picture of your whole project. It is better to set your sights lower and tie up all loose ends, rather than being too ambitious and not really coming to any definite conclusions.

Conclusions

This is a section of key importance for the quality of your dissertation.

The conclusions should be drawn from your methods and results. Do not try to make 'sensible' conclusions which exceed the scope of your study. It is better to have simple, logical, effective conclusions for which you can provide robust and appropriate evidence rather than make assumptions which over-step your evidence and consequently devalue your work. For this reason, you might also want to include in your conclusions a short evaluation of your methods and the quality of your results.

There are several good tips to keep in mind.

- Keep the conclusions straightforward. (i.e. "If X happens then Y is likely to result due to...").

- Refer back to the numbered section in the text which provides the evidence.

- Number the conclusions individually.

- Summarise your points rather than repeat previous text.

- Restrict your discussion to the implications of the conclusions.

- Your conclusions should summarise the main points without over-simplification.

Do not:

- add new data, information or opinions that you have not introduced earlier

- repeat your argument word for word from earlier sections

- be tempted to infer too many conclusions

- be too adventurous regarding the significance of your conclusions (better to understate the importance of your results and have the reader getting excited about its potential, than claiming too much without rigorous proof and face criticism when things do not work out as you have assumed).

A good set of conclusions will probably be the last significant piece of your work to be read by an examiner. For this reason the conclusions are likely to have a crucial effect on the examiner in the assessment of your abilities for original, critical, and logical thought.

For this reason, the conclusions should be clear, unambiguous, but restrained.

Recommendations

If you include this section at all (it is not mandatory), then it should be short, and very specific.

This section is useful, particularly in a short research project or academic review, where there are tight deadlines and/or limited resources for the full and detailed investigation of the topic.

FRANK RENNIE & KEITH SMYTH

It should not be used as an excuse simply to list all the things which you did not get round to doing!

There are a number of reasons why you should not include this section in your dissertation.

- It draws attention to the things you have left undone.

- It adds to the total word count (and you might be trying to cut down already).

- Unless you are very specific about future research options, it might sound vague and confused - not the image on which you are trying to end!

On the more positive side.

- It can show that you fully understand your project and know its limitations.

- It can point the way to illustrating the complexity of your project.

- It can serve as a useful lead to the possibility of a subsequent, more advanced study.

- If you are in any doubt about including this section, ask yourself is it really necessary?

References

Regardless of how long or short your work is going to be, you will need to include references to other sources of information, which might include:

- books

- academic papers in journals

- specific sites on the World Wide Web

- documents or papers in an archive

- official papers, such as Minutes of Local Authority committee meetings

- Government publications

- private papers.

There are several reasons why you will want to make references to other literature in the main text of your own study, primarily these are:

- to demonstrate that you are familiar with what others have said about your topic (and that you are not trying to re-invent the wheel)

- to quote evidence from other sources to substantiate (or challenge) your own evidence

- to qualify your opinions and demonstrate support from other studies to justify your opinions.

All of these references need to be able to be traced back to the original source, so it is vitally important that you cite these accurately.

One of the most common conventions for listing academic literature is known as the Harvard System, and a guide for using this is included on the companion website. Some disciplines (e.g. theology) have a different system for giving citations and listing references, but unless you are informed otherwise by your supervisor, you should use the Harvard System.

Broadly speaking, the author's surname and date of the

publication are listed in brackets within the text at the appropriate reference point, for example in the following extract:

Within Europe, there is no evidence that families who practice part-time farming in combination with other jobs have a lower household income than full-time farmers. In fact the reverse may be the case. (Bryden, 1987)

The bit in brackets (Bryden, 1987) is called the citation, and refers the reader to seek the more detailed paper by an author called Bryden which was published in 1987.

In the References section at the end of your dissertation, you are required to list ALL of the references which you have used to compile your dissertation. For example the reference above would be listed alphabetically as:

- Bryden, J.M., 1987, Crofting in the European Context. Scottish Geographical Magazine 103 No.2 pp. 100-4.

Textbooks are listed similarly, but with the mention of the name of the Publisher (and frequently the ISBN - International Standard Book Number) in place of the volume and page numbers of the article.

Internet sites should give the full URL, and also, to avoid ambiguity, the date on which you accessed the site (you might want to retain a print-out for further proof. For example, the reference:

- Lews Castle College (2015) Home Page. [Online] Available from: http://www.lews.uhi.ac.uk [Accessed: 7 July 2015]

This would be cited in the main text as:

(Lews Castle College, 2000)

More than one reference by the same author or organisation is listed in order of ascending date. References to authors who have published more than one piece of relevant work during the same year, would be referred to as 2000a, or 2000b, et cetera.

The main purpose of citing references is to allow other readers to trace back from your work to other relevant pieces of work, so that they can examine the evidence for themselves. In order to do this, you need to be 100% accurate in listing your references. Do not assume that something 'is obvious' to a reader, though it may seem obvious to you.

Try to be consistent and give as much information as possible.

Do not use footnotes, or other annotations in the text to explain your references. Your main text and the reference list should be all you need.

Check the reference lists in other journals and textbooks to compare their style and to understand how to construct your own reference list.

Start to compile your reference list right from the start of the project and add each new relevant reference as you finish reading it. Do not wait until near the end of your writing - you are almost certain to lose track of some references. Keep a copy (printed plus digital) of each updated version reference list as you complete it.

Some researchers simply use a word document to

compile their list of references while others use computer applications such as RefWorks to do the job. There is no 'right way' to do this, only ways which are easier and more suited to your own working style.

Appendices

This is a much misused section of dissertations and reports.

The appendix is **not** used to simply dump all the extra materials which you cannot fit into the text.

Use the appendices sparingly. Only include information which is really important to your study but which might seem to clutter up the main text by its inclusion.

Examples of this may be:

- a verbatim transcription of a particularly significant interview (not all of them!)

- a long table of statistical information which you have collected which is relevant to your study (and which you have explained in the text)

- a template of the questionnaire(s) which you have used to collect data

- reproductions (photocopies?) of particularly relevant documents, for example legal papers

- detailed maps of field work et cetera.

- Do not include letters, leaflets, posters, or hand-outs from any other organisations unless these are critical evidence to substantiate your opinions.

You may gather a lot of information in the course of your study, and frequently you cannot use all of it. There is a valuable skill to be learned in being able to edit, select, and prioritise the most valuable pieces of information which enable you to explain your particular topic.

If you put too much into the appendices, they are unlikely to be read fully, and your efforts will be wasted.

In Summary

Essential material should be in the main text, supporting evidence can be included as an appendix, but this should be used only for information which is highly relevant though subsidiary to your main discussion. If in doubt, leave it out.

Optional Activity

Visit the companion website
                www.etextbooks.ac.uk/dissertation
to view more resources.

Background Reading

Blaxter, Hughes, and Tight, (2006) - Chapters 8 and 9

FRANK RENNIE & KEITH SMYTH

REFERENCES

Bell, J. (2010) Doing your research project: a guide for first-time researchers in education, health and social science (5th Edition). Open University Press.

Blaxter, L., Hughes, C., and Tight, M. (2010) How to research (4th Edition). The Open University Press

Bryman, A. (2012) Social Research Methods (4th Edition) Oxford University Press.

Creswell, J. W. (2009) Research Design: Qualitative, Quantitative and Mixed Method Approaches. Sage Pub. (3rd Edition.)

Guba, E.G. and Lincoln, Y.S. (1994)Competing paradigms in qualitative research. In N.K. Denzin and Y.S. Lincoln (Eds.), Handbook of qualitative research methods (pp. 105-117). Thousand Oaks, California: Sage.

Hart, C. (1998) Doing a Literature Review: Releasing the Social Science Research Imagination. Sage Publications.

Higher Education Academy (2012) Guide to Undergraduate Dissertations in the Social Sciences. Available online at http://www.socscidiss.bham.ac.uk

Mather, A. S. and Ardern, R. J. (1981) An annotated bibliography of rural land use in the Highlands and Islands of Scotland, 193pp. O'Dell Memorial Monograph No. 9 Dept. of Geography, University of Aberdeen ISSN 0141-1454

Murray, R. (2002) How to write a thesis. Open University Press.

Ridley, D. (2012) The Literature Review: A Step-by-Step Guide for Students (2nd Edition). Sage.

Ritchie, J. and Lewis, J. (Eds.) (2013). Qualitative research practice: a guide for social science students and researchers. Sage.

Shaw, M.D. (2007) Mastering online research: a comprehensive guide to effective and efficient search strategies. Ohio: F+W Publications.

Stake, R.E. (1994). Case studies. In N.K. Denzin & Y.S. Lincoln (Eds.), Handbook of qualitative research methods (pp.236-247). Thousand Oaks, California: Sage.

Walliman, N. S. R. (2004) Your undergraduate dissertation: the essential guide for success. Sage Publications.

Printed in Great Britain
by Amazon

10705276R00068